TENNIS

SMART & SIMPLE

For Players and Coaches of All Levels and Ages

SOPHIE AMIACH

TENNIS
SMART & SIMPLE

For Players and Coaches of All Levels and Ages

"*Tennis Smart & Simple*" is published by New Chapter Press (www.NewChapterMedia.com) and is distributed by the Independent Publishers Group (www.IPGBook.com).

ISBN: 978-1950148004

For more information on this title or New Chapter Press, contact:
Randy Walker
1175 York Ave., Suite #3s New York, NY 10065
Rwalker@NewChapterMedia.com

Praise for Tennis Smart & Simple

"Clear, engaging and fun. Sophie's professional playing & broadcasting experience shines through: she explains the game with clarity and compelling storytelling. The QR videos are outstanding teaching aids that beautifully complement the text and images."

Martina Navratilova, Nine-time Wimbledon champion

"In Tennis Smart and Simple, my good friend Sophie Amiach captures the tennis experience in a refreshingly down-to-earth way, keeping things simple, real and easy to apply. This isn't a book you read once and put away - it's a road map you bring to the court and use every time you play."

Billie Jean King, Sports Icon and Equality Champion

"Genius is in simplicity and Sophie's book is exactly that"

Ivan Lendl, Three-time U.S. Open champion

"I've known Sophie for decades, first as a professional tennis player and now working beside her as we analyze Grand Slam events around the world. I have long been impressed with her clear-eyed, hard earned command of the sport. From fundamentals to advanced tactics, Sophie's insider know how, will help you play smarter and improve quickly. Tennis Smart & Simple is a gem."

Mary Carillo, 2026 International Tennis Hall of Famer

"Whether you're introducing beginners or refining a touring player, Tennis Smart & Simple is a toolbox you'll reach for every day. The step-by-step videos links make instruction simple, repeatable and adaptable for all ages and skill levels — a huge asset for teaching professionals and coaches.

Jimmy Arias, Former ATP World No. 5 and broadcaster

"As a former world No. 6 player who has been in the commentary booth for over a decade, I understand how important it is to break down complex shots into simple, explainable, and repeatable steps. This is where Sophie's professional playing and broadcasting experience shines through: she explains the game with clarity and compelling storytelling. And the QR codes videos are innovative, well-executed teaching aids that beautifully complement the text and images. Tennis Smart & Simple is a must have in your tennis bag."

Chanda Rubin, Former World No. 6 and broadcaster

"Practical, visual and immediately usable — that's Tennis Smart & Simple. Sophie breaks complex shots into simple, repeatable steps, and the linked videos through the QR codes make it easy for players, amateurs to professionals at every level to practice correctly and confidently. A must-have in your tennis bag for players and coaches."

Pam Shriver, International Tennis Hall of Famer and broadcaster

"As a former tour professional, I vouch for this instructive guide and the many pathways it offers to play your best. Consistent performance is built on the right habits, and Tennis Smart & Simple gives you the tools to do it. The exercises are enjoyable and effective, and the QR codes demos feel like having Sophie on court with you — expect noticeable improvements fast."

Katrina Adams, former WTA player, USTA President and broadcaster

"I have been fortunate to work alongside Sophie in the commentary booth over many years at WTA events. Her passion mixed with tennis IQ and EQ is a real asset to this wonderful sport of ours. Sophie's insights help players at every single level and importantly, the viewers at home understand and digest a match at the highest level. Sophie has always remained at the cusp in evolving at the same rapid rate of the evolution of this sport. She was a wonderful player, coach and now an incredible teacher of the game. Read... Watch... Learn... And improve! I continue to learn more about tennis every minute I sit beside her in the commentary box."

Alicia Molik, 2004 Olympic Bronze Medalist and broadcaster

"From one pro to another, I can truly say Sophie has poured her whole tennis life onto these pages. She's lived the tour, coached at the WTA level, taught countless players, and seen the game from every angle. That rare mix shines through in a way that makes *Tennis Smart & Simple* fun read. With her eye for detail, the clear photos, and the QR code videos, every drill and tactic comes alive. What makes this even more special is the sisterhood — one woman giving back to the game so others can grow. This is Sophie at her best, and it's a gift for every player, coach, and fan."

Zina Garrison, 1988 Olympic doubles gold medalist and broadcaster

"One of the most brilliant minds in tennis has chosen to share her experience with us-and we are all the better for it. Even the very best players must return to fundamentals when things aren't going their way. This book complete with QR code videos that provide instant visual guidance, is an invaluable resource that will elevate your game and make you a better tennis player."

Andrea Petkovic, Former World No. 9 and broadcaster

Special Words From 1983 Roland Garros Champion and World-Famous Singer Yannick Noah

"It feels like a lifetime since we were playing on the courts of the Nice Lawn Tennis Club in Nice, France—decades ago now. When you turn the pages of our professional careers and the lights finally go out, what truly remains? The friends. The brothers and sisters. The tennis family. Reading your book brought back a flood of memories. I even caught myself wondering—should I attempt a comeback? Or is it a little too late? (laughs). There were so many things back then that I didn't fully understand. You should have been my coach—my technical guide, my sparring partner, and of course, a true friend on the road. Now we've reached a stage in life where our mission is to pass on what we've learned. I'm genuinely impressed by the quality of your book. Today, it's all about sharing knowledge, and I'm certain that anyone

Yannick Noah with Sophie Amiach

who reads Tennis Smart & Simple will feel inspired and elevate their game. I know I will—I'm already eager to try a few adjustments, especially on my forehand (laughs). And the QR codes are a brilliant touch—I can't wait to get back on court and test it all out!"

Dedication

My friends who know me best use a wide range of adjectives to describe me: opinionated, energized, exuberant, impulsive, fun, competitive, embracing and sometimes annoying ☺.

They know that I love life, I live in the moment, and I'm deeply grateful for how fortunate my journey has been.

I also consider myself spiritual and my mother was my greatest spiritual guide. I miss her every day, and I always will. I feel her with me, always.

Sophie Amiach and her mother Rolande Cathala

So, I dedicate this book to her—

Rolande, ma chère et tendre Maman—

And to all my friends who've helped me along this amazing journey on Earth.

I'm often heard saying: **"I'm jazzed by life."** And I hope this book helps jazz up yours, too.

Keep swinging at that fuzzy yellow ball.

And never forget…

HAVE FUN OUT THERE!

Contents

From The Author

My name is Sophie Amiach, and I love tennis. Growing up in Nice, France, I believed tennis was in my blood. Not only did I attend Roland Garros High School, but I also trained at the Stade Roland Garros in Paris—and eventually had the honor of competing there in the French Open. Did I mention my father's name was Roland and my mother's, Rolande? Ah, destiny.

Sophie Amiach in action

I wrote *Tennis Smart & Simple* to share the benefits of my experience as a professional player, student, teacher, coach, and now, TV and radio commentator. My hope is that players and coaches of all ages and skill levels—amateurs and professionals alike—will find this book and its QR-coded videos to be a valuable resource for strengthening both their game and their understanding of it.

As for my journey, my professional career on the WTA Tour spanned 15 years (1980–1995). I achieved a career-high rankings of No. 57 in singles, No. 62 in doubles, and No. 5 in France. In 1980, I reached the doubles quarterfinals at the Australian Open, and in 1984, I made it to the singles quarterfinals there—facing none other than Chris Evert.

After a serious injury caused my ranking to plummet from No. 110 to No. 576, I considered ending my career. But destiny stepped in again—this time in the form of one of the greatest gifts of my life: meeting and being coached by Billie Jean King.

Amiach with Billie Jean King

My best friend, CVG, worked at World TeamTennis in Chicago, which was founded by Billie Jean and run by both her life time partner and now wife, Ilana Kloss. When CVG told Billie I was thinking of quitting, she responded, "End her career at 24? That's when you start a career." And just like that, my lucky star appeared. Billie coached me for the next two years—entirely free of charge.

I vividly remember our first day on court together at the Midtown Tennis Club, which was owned by former USTA President Alan Schwartz. He and Club Director Pat Freebody generously let me train there gratis—something I deeply appreciated, as I was completely broke at the time. Billie and I were supposed to just hit a few balls, but three minutes in, she stopped and said, "I want you to give me a lesson."

I was floored. "A lesson? You want a lesson from me? You were No. 1 in the world and won 39 major titles."

"I know," she said. "But I still want you to teach me."

It was her way of testing me—and it worked. I quickly realized I had no idea how to explain tennis. I had just done it all those years. That moment opened my eyes.

Starting over from the bottom, I worked my way back through the ITF circuit—those small, often obscure tournaments around the world where players claw their way up the rankings. It's the ultimate test of resolve. Imagine going back to middle school after earning a master's degree. Trust me—playing in Scandinavia in January is a far cry from the balmy courts of the Australian Open.

Left to right: Pierre and Nicole Filipone, Sophie Amiach, Bernard and Brigitte Paul

But I pushed through and eventually broke back near the Top 100, which gave me another chance to get direct entry into the four Majors: the Australian Open, the French Open (Roland Garros), Wimbledon, and the US Open. It took everything I had—and I couldn't have done it without Billie Jean's mentorship and generosity. She didn't just help me play better; she helped me understand the game.

In 1987, I was honored to be nominated for WTA Comeback Player of the Year—an acknowledgment of my dedication and perseverance. So how did I manage to compete at the highest level—and even reach the quarterfinals of a major—without being able to articulate the basics? Simple: I had two incredible coaches. Nicole Filippone gave me a solid foundation, and Bernard Paul was a master tactician.

But it wasn't until Billie came along that I truly learned how to understand my mistakes, stay mentally tough, and manage pressure.

That's not to say my earlier coaches weren't brilliant—they absolutely were—but Billie taught me how to connect knowledge to expression. With Billie's guidance, I became a better player, a better teacher, and a more present, joyful human being. That ability to stay in the moment—to enjoy the process—is what I now believe to be the real secret to success, both on and off the court.

I love what I do, and I still love the game.

Acknowledgements

Writing a book is a lot like playing a tennis match—success often comes down to teamwork. I've been incredibly lucky to have wonderful people around me throughout this journey.

First and foremost, thank you to my wife, Donna, for her unwavering love, support, and always having my back. I'm also deeply grateful to the incredible team of friends who played a role in this project. Your support not only helped bring this book to life—it deepened our bonds of friendship.

Sophie and her wife Donna Shea

A special thank you to Kevin Skinner for editing my French-English writing—probably the biggest task of all!; to Cristina in Florida for her valuable input, and for being the best dentist EVER, giving me my best smile. I also want to thank the Polo Club in Boca Raton and their Tennis Director, Laurent Leclerc, for their generous use of their facility in filming the videos that accompany this book. To my friends Pat and Heather for their valuable input, to Denise "DD" for her creative mind and friendship, to Andrew for his patience directing and editing the videos and pictures. To my sponsors Don Lock (the most incredible master watch maker), Master Athletics for their generous support and Shoreline Pickleball for their tremendous help as well.

Many thanks to Karine Quentrec for her help with those videos—and even more so for her friendship. To my amazing hosts in Florida, Donna and Kathy, thank you for your kindness, friendship, support, and warm hospitality.

At the finish line for the last and crucial editing, a huge thank you to Maggie whose expertise, knowledge and professionalism gave more flair and depth to the book.

Don Lock watch maker www.dloke.com
Master Athletics https://www.master-athletics.com
Shoreline Pickleball https://www.shorelinepickleball.com
Dr. Cristina M. Kuhnel www.kuhneldentistry.com

Last, but most certainly not least, my sincere gratitude goes to Billie Jean King. Without her influence and generosity, I might have left tennis behind at 24—and missed out on all the joy this sport has brought into my life. Merci, Billie!

PART I :

Technique & Shots

Why Start With Technique?

Because sound technique = consistent results.

Before you even step onto the court, your first move should be to find a local professional—someone at a tennis club, a recreation center, or your own coach. Have a conversation about their philosophy: how they'll help you become a better tennis player or elevate your current game. Ask questions. Look for thoughtful answers. If they talk about "fundamentals," you're off to a great start.

In every sport, fundamentals begin with proper, simple technique—and tennis is no exception. A solid technique becomes especially valuable under pressure. It's what holds up during high-stress moments and leads to steady improvement and more consistent results.

So, what exactly is a simple technique?

I'd describe it as a flawless technique. Some of the best examples come from players like Novak Djokovic, Roger Federer, Serena Williams and Jessica Pegula. What they have in common is efficiency: they aren't doing too much before making contact with the ball. Their timing is impeccable, their point of contact clean and precise. That's how they execute those beautifully consistent shots.

When you're working with your tennis pro, here's another key question to ask: "Is a one-handed or two-handed backhand better for my game?"

A good coach might say, "Either one," or "It doesn't matter." But the best answer is: "It depends—on your ability, body mechanics, movement, speed, and personal preference."

If there were only one right way to hit a backhand, we'd all use it—and we'd all look the same doing it. What really matters is YOU. A great coach will say, "Let me see you hit a few first, and we'll figure out what works best for YOU."

Back To Fundamentals—Let's Talk Physics

To consistently hit the ball over the net from behind the baseline, you have two basic options:

1. Open the face of the racket toward the sky, get the racket head below the ball, and swing with your racket head with an upward and forward motion.

2. Use a brushing, low-to-high motion at impact to create arc and spin—also known as topspin.

While both approaches can work, brushing the ball for topspin is the safer, more consistent one. Topspin adds weight to the ball, helping gravity bring it down inside the court and minimizing depth errors.

For generating topspin, I recommend:

- A western grip for forehands and both one- and two-handed backhands.
- A continental grip can also work well on a backhand two-hander.
- For slices or underspin, continental or eastern grips are your best bet.

At the net on your volleys use a continental grip as well.

The key to topspin is getting the racket head below the ball before contact. This requires your wrist to drop in the prep phase, automatically lowering the racket head. How you achieve that position depends on you—some players use a big loop or "C" shape in their swing, others prefer a shorter loop or even a straight takeback. Again, it's about what works best for your body and game.

But one thing is certain: in slow-motion footage of the pros, you'll always see that racket head drop. Rafael Nadal drops it deeply to create heavy topspin; Karolina Pliskova less so, for a flatter shot. The technique may vary, but the principle stays the same.

What About The Follow-Through?

There are two primary finishes:

- Across your opposite shoulder
- Over your head (like Rafael Nadal)

Your follow-through reflects your intent—more topspin, deeper balls, shorter angles—and your personal preference.

The most important thing? You should feel balanced and stable through your finish. For two-handed backhands, finishing with both arms over your opposite shoulder usually gives you better control. Want to study beautiful one-handers? Look up Justine Henin, Amélie Mauresmo, Carla Suárez Navarro, Roger Federer, Stefanos Tsitsipas, Denis Shapovalov, Stan Wawrinka, and Dominic Thiem. You'll notice something they all do: **they separate their arms at contact for balance and control.**

As you progress and gain a better feel for your shot mechanics, you'll also begin to control how you want to play—including how deep or short your shots land.

You'll get **more depth when you fully extend your arm at the moment of impact**. On the flip side, shorter strokes with **less extension and less racket-head follow-through** will result in the ball landing closer to the net. It's all about how you finish the shot. A great drill to practice this: Start in front of the net and throw a ball underhand toward the back fence, extending your arm fully upward and forward, finishing around shoulder height.

Then, try the opposite: toss the ball underhand again, but this time let your arm drop below your navel and stop short. Notice the difference in how far the ball travels. One lands deep, the other short. That's the power of extension.

Once you've practiced this a few times, grab your racket, drop the ball with your non-hitting hand, let it bounce, and try hitting it with your racket while mimicking both the long and short throwing motions.

Here's a visualization that helps: Imagine your racket as an extension of your forearm and hand. To hit deeper, let your forearm and hand "push through" the ball with a longer extension. For shorter shots, keep the stroke shorter with less extension but still finish clean. Both variations have value—you'll use them depending on your strategy and position on the court.

The Split Step

Now let's talk about one of the **most important—but often overlooked—fundamentals in tennis**: the **split step**.

The split step is a small, explosive hop that helps you get into the best possible position to hit your next shot. It sets your body weight forward—onto the balls of your feet—with your heels slightly off the ground, so you're ready to move in any direction *immediately*. Think of it as a mini jumpstart.

Here's the key: **You must execute the split step just *before* your opponent makes contact with the ball.**

This timing allows your body to react instantly, giving you that extra edge in speed and positioning.

Why is the split step (hop) so essential?

Because tennis is all about fast, explosive movement. If you're standing flat-footed or with your weight on your heels, you'll lose valuable time just shifting into motion. The split step skips that delay, putting you in a ready-to-react position right away. Even a fraction of a second—just one-tenth—can make a difference between a great and poor shot.

Your **first step** after the split often determines whether you'll be in position to hit a quality shot.

Now, keep in mind: you won't always have time to recover fully between shots. Sometimes, you'll be hurrying back to center or still be off-balance when your opponent strikes the ball. Split-step anyway. No matter where you are on the court when your opponent is about to make contact, it's better to be ready than caught flat-footed.

Want To See It In Action?

Watch a professional match and choose one player to focus on. Every time their opponent hits the ball, observe how they execute their split step. Pay close attention to the timing—just before the other player makes contact. You'll start to notice that it's almost instinctive. Now try it yourself during practice. With repetition, your split step will become second nature—and your game will improve because of it.

The Power of Pace

Another essential element of tennis is learning to hit shots that can truly *hurt* your opponent—not physically, of course (although in the long run it might), but strategically. I often hear players say, "I want to hit harder." But what does that really mean?

What they're really asking for is more **power**—also known as **pace**. Pace refers to the speed and weight—or "heaviness"—of the ball as it moves through the air. A ball with real pace enables you to hit more winners, forces your opponent into rushed reactions, weaker returns, or outright errors.

So how do you generate pace?

It all starts with sound technique and, perhaps surprisingly, a **relaxed arm**, especially just before contact. The biggest contribution to power is **elasticity**—that whip-like, fluid quality in your arm. And elasticity requires relaxation. A tense arm can't whip. A relaxed one can accelerate through impact quickly and powerfully.

It's not about muscling the ball. Think of it like throwing a baseball or a football. Watch how quarterbacks and pitchers keep their throwing arms and ultimately their hand loose until the last moment—they're generating maximum acceleration through relaxation, not brute force.

Since your racket is an extension of your arm and hand, the more relaxed your hitting arm and hand are, the more speed and energy you'll transfer into the ball at the moment of contact. Focus less on swinging *hard,* and more on swinging *fast*—with loose, fluid mechanics. That's how you build real power.

The Serve

So, what exactly makes a *good* serve?

It's not just about blasting aces—although those are nice. A great serve is about **consistency, placement and control**, not just speed. The ability to hit a high percentage of first serves, target different spots in the service box, and deliver a reliable second serve with depth and spin—that's what makes a serve effective.

Even more important than aces are **free points**—winning quick points that keep your service games short and stress-free. Free points come in a few forms:

- A serve your opponent can't touch (ACE)
- A serve they returned ineffectively (SERVICE WINNER)
- A weak return that sets you up for an easy winner (PUT-AWAY)

The best servers in the world master all of these. Serena Williams and Roger Federer are prime examples. They don't just serve hard and with pace—they serve smart, with purpose and variety.

Some might also mention Novak Djokovic. Earlier in his career, his serve was less effective—his racket face stayed too open before contact. But to his credit, Novak adjusted. He refined his motion, improving his technique, consistency and power. That kind of evolution is a lesson in itself.

For your own serve, I recommend using a **continental grip**—ideal for flat and slice serves—as your foundation. Some players also experiment with an **eastern grip** to find more comfort and spin, especially for the kick serve.

Take some time to study slow-motion footage of the greats. Watch how Serena and Roger approach their service motion. Notice how **relaxed** their arms remain throughout. Their movements are fluid, their shoulders tilt naturally (more pronounced on Federer), and their timing is impeccable. Federer's toss and upper body rotation, in particular, are absolutely beautiful to watch—like poetry in motion.

Their arms stay loose, their elbows bend with ease, and they use that elasticity to whip through the ball, generating power and placement without unnecessary tension.

One final note:

While big servers like John Isner may come to mind, it's important to remember that his 6'10" frame gives him unique advantages. Unless you share his height, focus on players closer to your own build—like Roger and Serena. Their techniques are more relatable and repeatable for most players.

Two More Keys to a Great Serve: Position and Toss

In addition to motion and power, two often overlooked elements of a great serve are your **serve position** and your

ball toss. These foundational pieces are critical to building a consistent, effective serve.

Serve Position

Your stance should be **simple, balanced, and stable**—giving you maximum reach and allowing you to serve with ease and control.

If you're **right-handed**:

- Point your **left foot** (and big toe) toward the **right net post**.

- Your **right foot** should be almost parallel to the baseline.

- Keep your feet **shoulder-width apart**—this gives you a strong, balanced base.

A good test: if someone were to come up and push you, you should feel **anchored**. Solid. Grounded. Now imagine a rope stretched from your **right big toe to your left big toe**, continuing across the net. That rope would point toward the **center of the service box**—the way your racket head is facing at impact will direct where your serve will land in the box.

If you're **left-handed**, reverse the setup:

- Your **right foot** (and big toe) points toward the **left net post**

- Your **left foot** stays almost parallel to the baseline.

Once you've tossed the ball, you'll step into the serve. For right-handers, that means your right foot will step in just slightly to the right of, or alongside, your left foot, with your knees bent and ready to push upward toward the ball. That leg drive is key—it helps you push up from the bend in your knees to reach the peak of your toss and increases your margin over the net. Gaël Monfils often begins his motion with his feet closer together and his knees bent from the start. On other days, he'll bring his right foot in after the toss. While that style works for a few, it's less common among the game's most consistent servers.

Here's the takeaway: While there are exceptions, **the best servers in the world keep it simple**. Fewer moving parts means **better timing and more consistent contact**. Complexity invites errors. Simplicity brings consistency and results.

The Underarm Serve

Use it and don't feel bad about it, I never understood why it wasn't used more on the men's tour. Players like Nadal and Medvedev and so many more will stand so far behind the baseline to return serves that it is such a great serve to hit. Would you not hit a dropshot because your opponent is standing far from the baseline? Of course not, in my opinion it is the exact same strategy. Again don't be afraid to use it.

The Toss (Part A): Technique

Your toss is the heartbeat of your serve. A **consistent toss** allows for a **repeatable motion**—which leads to cleaner contact and better results.

Here's how to create that consistency: Keep your **tossing arm straight**—no wrist flicking or forearm bending.

Hold the ball level of your phalanges/fingertips, resting it just above your palm. Your thumb should apply slightly more pressure.

Move your arm **along one continuous path**, from thigh to eye level, and **release the ball between your shoulder and eyes**.

As you release, **fully extend your arm upward**, keeping your fingers pointing to the sky.

Bonus tip: Keep your tossing arm **extended** as long as possible. Many players drop their tossing arm too early, which can throw them off balance at point of contact.

Think of your toss like sending the ball up a **tight tunnel** toward your target. A great way to feel this motion is to start with your tossing hand **touching your thigh**. Keep it in line with your leg as you raise it. The more controlled the path, the more reliable the toss.

The Toss (Part B): Where Should It Land?

Even though your **first and second serve tosses** might vary slightly, each one should be **consistent for the type of serve you're executing**. You want your toss to **match your intention**, not to tip off your opponent. Whether you're hitting flat, slice, or kick serves, the toss should land in a spot that lets you:

- **Apply The Right Spin**
- **Target different areas** of the service box

- **Keep your opponent guessing**

On **second serves**, many players favor a **kick serve**. For right-handed players, this usually means tossing the ball slightly to the **left and behind your head**. For left-handers, it's the opposite.

Kick serves create more height, more spin, and more margin over the net. Use a **low-to-high racket path**, with quick wrist action and **pronation** at full extension.

To visualize toss placement, **imagine a clock face**:

- For **right-handers**:
    - Toss to **1–2 o'clock** for a flat or slice serve
    - Toss to **7–8 o'clock** for a kick serve, swinging diagonally back toward 1–2

- For **left-handers**:
    - Toss to **10–11 o'clock** for a flat or slice
    - Toss to **4–5 o'clock** for a kick serve, finishing across to 10–11

- To create topspin on a kick serve, strike the ball between **7 and 8**, finishing diagonally toward **1**.

- You can even think of the **ball itself as a clock**:

Finally, at impact, **swing your racket toward your intended target**—whether you're going up the T, out wide, or into the body. **The way your racket head is facing at impact dictates where your ball will land on the opposite side and that applies to all the shots in tennis.**

News Flash: The Serve Is the Easiest Stroke to Practice

Unlike other shots, the serve doesn't require a partner. You just need a **basket of balls**, some space, and the **desire to improve**.

Drill: Mastering Your Toss

1. Place a **flat target** on the court where you want your toss to land for both first and second serves.
2. Practice tossing the ball repeatedly—**don't hit it yet**—and make sure both arms are starting at about the same time. Keep working on your toss until you can land the toss on your target with consistency.
3. Once it becomes second nature, go for it serve it out!

The more consistent your toss, the more confident and effective your entire serve becomes.

Kick serve Righthanded players

Racket head makes contact between 7 & 8 finishing between 1 & 2 With a low to high and forward movement at impact towards the target

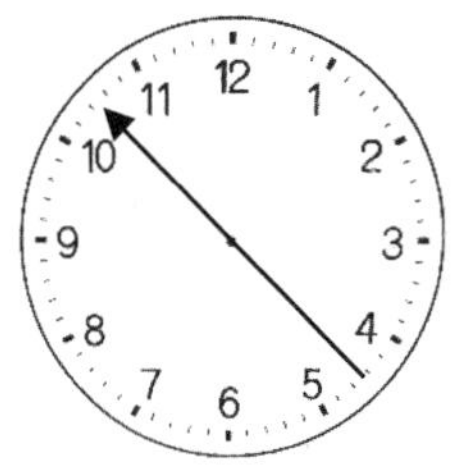

Kick serve Lefthanded players

Racket head makes contact between 4 & 5 finishing between 10 & 11 with a low to high and forward movement at impact towards the target

<u>Righthanded Players</u> **Flat serve**
Toss and hit at 1 with the racket face parallel to the ball at impact
<u>Righthanded Players</u> **Slice serve**
Toss and hit between 1 & 2 with the racket face making contact on the right side of the ball to create the slice

<u>Lefthanded Player's</u> **Flat serve**
Toss and hit at 11 with the racket face parallel to the ball at impact
<u>Lefthanded Player's</u> **Slice serve**
Toss and hit between 10 & 11 with the racket face making contact on the left side of the ball to create the slice

The Wrist Snap

In order to gain better control and exaggerate the amount of spin on the kick serve, good technique requires pronation and a snap of the wrist at impact. The butt of your racket should be facing the fence behind you to achieve the best wrist pronation/snap when striking the ball. In order to properly master this technique, it is All. About. Repetition. Get a bucket of balls, and hit two to four buckets a day, working on your first and second serves, in multiple directions, with various spins. Dedicating time to your game is important in order to achieve the competency you seek.

Drill: Chart Your Percentages

Play a full set without an opponent, serving only. During the set, chart your first and second serve percentages, as well as any double faults. Retake any toss that does not land in the correct strike zone.

Volleys

Classic forehand and backhand volleys are executed using a short swing and a firm wrist at impact.

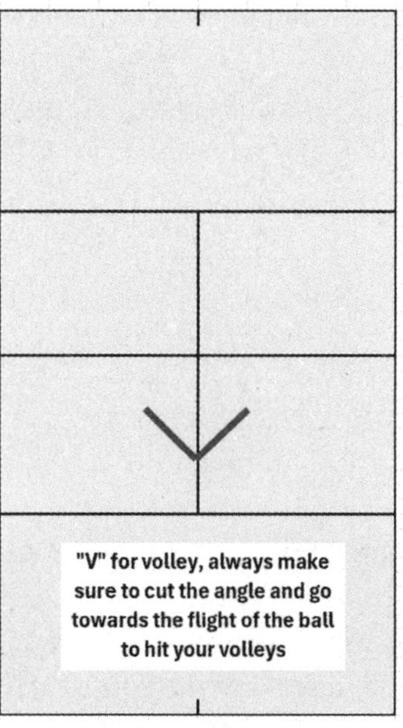

Always move diagonally to the ball along an imaginary "V" from each of your toes towards the net.

1/ to cut the angle

2/ to hit the ball as high as possible trying to hit the ball above the level of the net as often as possible. Also avoid your racket head going behind your shoulder also creating a "V" from your hand and racket towards impact with classic volleys. When attempting to volley a ball that is positioned below the level of the net, be sure to slightly open the face of your racket, blocking your wrist at impact, so as to allow the ball to clear the net, rather than end up in the net.

Use a one-handed backhand volley whenever possible—even if you typically use a two-handed backhand groundstroke. A one-handed volley allows for greater reach and more effective net play, especially when executing a drop shot volley. The drop shot volley is all about feel. One crucial aspect to remember: DO NOT SCOOP THE BALL, as the ball will stick to your strings and end up on your side of the net. Instead, stop your racket head at impact, while slightly opening the face of your racket.

Drill: Placing Your Volley

While practicing with a friend, teaching professional, or using a ball machine, have balls hit towards you at different heights, spin, and pace. Work repetitively on setting targets where you want your volleys to land.

The Topspin Swing Volley

To hit an effective topspin swing volley, timing is everything. Start by lowering your racket head—let your wrist drop below the level of the ball. Then, swing quickly from low to high, brushing up with your racket head to generate the desired topspin. Aim to make contact just above net level to get that nice low-to-high action.

On the backhand side, this shot is much easier with two hands, so if you've got a two-handed backhand, this is your time to shine. A one-handed swing volley, on the other hand, is rarely seen—it's one of the toughest shots in tennis as it requires great upper body strength. That said, I've watched the likes of Roger Federer, Stefanos Tsitsipas and Grigor Dimitrov pull it off with elegance. While it's not impossible, I highly recommend sticking with a two-handed high volley and if you play with a one-hander use the one-handed classic volley—unless, of course, you're chasing greatness.

The Drop Shot

To execute an effective drop shot, I recommend using the same technique as you would for a classic forehand or backhand volley drop shot. If you have a two-handed backhand and want better control, try learning to hit the drop shot with one hand. (While you're at it, it's a great time to develop a one-handed slice/underspin backhand groundstrokes.)

Drop shots taken off the bounce require the same fundamentals as drop shot volleys: use a slightly open racket face and keep your wrist firm at impact. And for emphasis—absolutely no scooping. Another key detail: resist the urge to follow through. Instead, stop your racket head right at the point of contact.

It's always easier to hit a drop shot when the ball is coming at you with some pace. You can use your opponent's power to your advantage—just block the shot with a firm wrist and let the ball come off your strings with soft precision. To maintain control, stop your racket at impact with a slightly angled face. If you stop too soon, the ball won't make it over the net. If you open your racket face too much, the ball will sail too high. (Yes, here comes the friendly reminder again: do not scoop the ball.)

The goal of a great drop shot is simple—get the ball just high enough to clear the net and land it short enough on your opponent's side so they can't reach it. If your drop shot floats too high or lands too deep, you're basically handing your opponent the chance to run it down—and possibly hit a winner.

Drill: Practice, Practice and Keep Practicing

Get a hitting partner, your own coach or a ball machine, to feed you a variety of shots, and using the drop shot technique described above, practice hitting ball after ball until it starts to feel natural. Repetition is key.

One thing Billie Jean King used to say to me—and it's stuck with me ever since—was:

"Once you've repeated a shot so many times that it starts to feel boring... that means you've got it."

Brilliant. And so true.

Overhead

Overheads are all about technique and footwork. Without proper adjustment steps, it's tough to get into the right position to execute the shot cleanly.

You've probably heard coaches shout, "Get under the ball! Get under the ball!" But that advice can be a little misleading. You don't actually want to be directly under the ball. Instead, position yourself so the ball is slightly in front and just off to the side—right side if you're right-handed, left side if you're left-handed. This allows your arm to extend fully and naturally, much like when you serve, so you can strike the ball at the ideal contact point.

When you set yourself up directly underneath the ball, your head tends to get in the way of your swing. But when you stand beside the ball—rather than under it—you give yourself more space for your arm to move through and toward the ball, along with better balance and a much cleaner path to contact.

Bouncing Overheads

This shot is trickier because you're farther from the net and the ball has to travel a greater distance to reach the other side. That means you'll need to hit the ball as high as possible after the bounce with more precision.

Set yourself farther back from the ball and give yourself more space between you and the ball—it will move slightly toward you after the bounce. When you make contact, be sure your upper body is upright and driving forward. Think ballerina, not bobblehead.

Billie Jean King used to say: *keep your posture like a dancer*. Even the great Coco Gauff, for example, sometimes bows too early on her serve—and that collapse often results in balls going into the net. So, keep that chest high and spine tall when smashing overheads at the net or after the bounce.

The Lob

The lob is one of the most underrated offensive weapons in tennis

Yes, it's often used defensively—but don't forget: a lob can also be a fantastic passing shot and a strong offensive play in doubles. Too many players underestimate its value when attacking, particularly when the net player keeps creeping closer and closer to the net. A well-placed lob can punish that kind of aggressive positioning at the net in an instant.

To master the lob, start by reading your opponent's court position:

- Are they hugging the net? That's your green light.
- Are they right- or left-handed? Then aim your lob to the opposite side of their dominant arm—meaning lob to the left side of a right-hander, or the right side of a lefty. This forces them into a more awkward—and often weaker—backhand high volley.

One of the greatest examples of strategic lobbing? Chris Evert vs. Martina Navratilova. They faced each other 80 times, including 60 finals! Evert, ever the tactician, would relentlessly lob to Martina's right side, exposing the left-hander's weaker backhand high volley. And wow—did that lob ever work.

On the men's side, Andre Agassi was a magician with the on-the-run top-spin lob. Sprinting full speed, he'd flick the ball low to high with so much spin and disguise that even the tallest net-rushers couldn't reach it. Carlos Alcaraz (a.k.a. "Carlito") and Ons Jabeur (nicknamed "The Minister of Happiness") are both brilliant at the modern offensive lob—it's part artistry, part strategy.

In doubles, try using the lob as a return of serve—especially over the net player. Slightly open your racket face at impact, block your wrist and let the server's pace do the work. It's effective, it's smart… and it's wildly underused, even at the pro level. One of my biggest pet peeves? How rarely is this play seen in high-level doubles—despite how often it could flip a point or even change the outcome of a match.

Drill: Overhead & Lob Live Ball Practice

This is one of my favorite drills—and a great way to build both consistency and control.

1. **Set up** with one player at the net (about 3 feet inside the service line) and the other at the baseline- first on the deuce side, then the ad side.

2. The net player works **only on overheads**, while the baseline player hits **only lobs**.

3. After every overhead, the net player must **recover forward** with proper footwork before the next shot. These adjustment steps are key to developing fluid movement and preparation.

4. Once comfortable, mix it up: The lobber can start blending in **groundstrokes** with lobs.

5. The net player can begin practicing **volleys and overheads in combination**.

The goal is simple: **repeat, refine and react**. Focus on **footwork, placement and rhythm**. Over time, both your overheads and lobs will become far more dependable—and dangerous.

Positioning During a Groundstroke Rally

Have I mentioned geometry yet? I'm pretty sure I have. 😉 Well, here's a perfect example of why geometry matters in tennis.

When rallying from the baseline, **your recovery path after hitting a shot should set you up diagonally—about one foot off the center line**, ideally diagonally in line with where your last shot landed on the other side. Why? Because **this puts you roughly equidistance from the two most likely shots your opponent might hit: a crosscourt or a down-the-line shot.**

A crosscourt shot travels on an angle and pulls away from you after the bounce, making it harder to reach. It keeps moving away. A down-the-line shot, on the other hand, travels in a straight line—and doesn't "escape" as quickly after the bounce as it continues its straight path. So, by recovering diagonally and slightly off-center, you put yourself in the smartest position possible. You're balanced, centered, and ready to chase down either angle with equal efficiency.

Approaching The Net

When you're coming forward, the geometry flips. You'll need to **mirror the direction of your approach shot**. If you are approaching crosscourt, your net position should be facing and aligned with wherever your approach shot lands—because the fastest passing shot your opponent can hit is **down the line**. (The term down the line means hitting straight to the right or left side of the court close to the side line but NEVER aiming on the line, give yourself a 1 to 2 foot margin.)

Why is that important? Because **straight shots travel faster** than those hit on an angle. A crosscourt pass travels longer to reach the intended target (when standing at the net), giving you more time to react. That's why players like **Billie Jean King** would say, "Cut the angle." Whether you're moving to intercept a volley or chasing a passing shot, your footwork should take you **diagonally forward**—never sideways—toward the bounce of the ball if you are hitting groundstrokes from the baseline or towards the flight of the ball when you are standing at the net hitting volleys.

At the net, if your opponent hits a crosscourt pass, moving diagonally allows you to **meet the ball early**, and more importantly, **higher in the air**. This gives you a better margin over the net and more control. The goal? Always hit your volleys at the **highest possible point**. The higher your point of contact with your racket head, the easier it is to be aggressive—and the fewer mistakes you'll make.

Approach Shot Strategy

Where should you hit your approach shot? Back to geometry.

A crosscourt approach means you'll have to cover more ground to get into position at the net and prepare for your opponent's passing shot. Why? Because you need to set yourself up at an equal distance from all of your opponent's passing shot options. That means mirroring your approach shot with your body placement at the net—

ready for the pass down the line, the crosscourt pass, or the lob—while keeping in mind that the down-the-line pass is the fastest, since it travels in a straight line.

A down-the-line approach, however, gets you to your ideal net position faster because, once again, you need to mirror your approach shot with your body placement at the net. It's a shorter path from where you hit your approach to where you need to be to cover your opponent's passing shot options—especially the down-the-line pass. That's why the down-the-line approach is often the more efficient and strategic choice, particularly when you're trying to close in on the net quickly.

Net Game Essentials

So what makes a great volley? It all starts with the **transition ball**—the shot you hit right after your approach shot or serve, if you are executing a serve and volley sequence before hitting your next shot, might it be a half volley or a volley.

Legendary net players like **Billie Jean King, Martina Navratilova, Roger Federer and Stefan Edberg** all knew that the transition ball was **crucial**. If you execute it well, you set yourself up to control the net. If you hit it poorly, you put yourself on defense.

Here's how to handle it:

- **Footwork** is everything. Use a **split step/hop** slightly before your opponent makes contact and always mirror your last shot's direction with your **body position** at the net.

- Think of yourself like a **train entering a station**—you briefly pause to pick up the "passenger" (the ball), then accelerate again toward your destination (net position).

- Your recovery position after an approach shot should be about **3 feet inside the service line**, slightly off-center in the direction of your approach shot.

Once your opponent makes contact, you MUST split step—**no matter where you are**. This lets you react explosively to the passing shot, whether it's down the line, crosscourt or a lob.

Serve-and-Volley Positioning

When serving and volleying, always **mirror the direction of your serve**. If you serve wide, for example, face in that direction as you move forward. Why? Because most players will return a wide serve **down the line**, not crosscourt as they'll most likely be late to making contact with the ball.

Remember, your opponent has **four return options**:

1. Down-the-line

2. Cross court

3. Lob

4. Low return at your feet for you to hit a half-volley

If the ball is high, finish the point with a put away volley or an overhead aiming for an angle.

If their return is low or you have to hit a half-volley, play it **deep down the line** to give yourself a chance to move forward and prepare for the next shot. Going crosscourt with a low volley gives your opponent **too much angle** and forces you to reposition more dramatically again as you have to mirror your last ball. So, down-the-line is the smarter, more compact option.

Split Step Reminder

Let's say it one more time (because it's that important): **Always split step before your opponent makes contact.** Whether you're rallying, approaching the net, or going to serve and volley, the split step prepares you to **explode in any direction**.

No split step = no reaction time.

Train your body to **split step instinctively**. It's the key to turning good court positioning into great results.

Drill: Shadow Work – Approach & Serve-and-Volley

Try this simple but powerful **shadow drill** on your own—no partner or court required:

1. **Start by shadowing** an approach shot or a serve-and-volley sequence.

2. If you're approaching, **split step**, then hit your "approach shot." If you're executing a serve and volley, **hit your serve**, then **sprint forward immediately**.

3. After the approach or serve, **position your body** so you're facing the direction your ball would travel—this is called **mirroring** your shot.

4. **Split step before your imaginary opponent makes contact.**

5. Hit your **transition shot**—the first ball after your approach or serve.

6. Move forward about 3 feet. **Split step again.**

7. Shadow hit another shot as a **put away or winner.**

Voilà! Rinse and repeat. Once you're confident, practice the sequence in live drills with a coach or hitting partner.

Return of Serve

A solid return starts with **great groundstroke technique**, but your **reaction time and ball recognition** are what elevate your return game.

The return of serve depends on two things:

- **How well you see the ball**
- **How quickly you react to it**

There are countless videos and tools online to help train both. Use them! Modern champions like **Andre Agassi, Novak Djokovic, Daniil Medvedev, Serena Williams, Victoria Azarenka, Aryna Sabalenka, Jessica Pegula** and **Iga Świątek** all excel at returning. It's no coincidence—they've practiced it obsessively.

Key Tips For Returning:

- **Split step just before your opponent makes contact.**
- **Shorten your swing**, especially on fast serves.
- **Pick a target** *before* the serve is hit and **commit** to it.
- Aim for safe zones—inside the sidelines and baseline—to allow margin for error.

Pro tip: A **down-the-line return** is often the most effective—it travels straight, takes time away from the server, and **lands at the farthest point on the court from the server**. A down-the-middle serve takes away angles on your opponent's return and can also jam them

Returning Specific Serves

Kick Serve

- If the ball kicks high, you have two options:

  - **Move forward** and take the ball early before it climbs above your shoulder height with the kick.

  - **Step back**, let the ball drop after the kick, and hit it at a more comfortable height.

Slice Serve

- For a right-handed opponent, the ball will swing out to your **right, opposite from a lefty**.
- Move **toward the bounce**, not sideways—**cut off the angle** early to take away the spin's effect.

Flat Serve

- Comes fast and straight.
- **Shorten your swing**, keep your **wrist firm**, and **block** the ball cleanly.
- Think of yourself as a **wall**—redirect the pace rather than generating your own.

Surprise Return: The Drop Shot

Rarely used, but highly effective when done well. The key? **Feel.** Learn to absorb the pace of a hard first serve or handle the spin of a second serve with control. Practice drop shot returns until they become instinctual.

Ons Jabeur, one of the most creative players on tour, often uses the **drop shot return** to throw off rhythm and steal free points. Watch her. Learn from her. Then hit thousands of drop shot returns until it becomes second nature. (*For drop shot technique, refer back to our earlier chapter.*)

Slice vs. Underspin or Backspin

Many players think these are the same.
They're not.

Slice Backhand (Right-Handed Player)

- Creates **side spin**—the ball rotates, and curves **left to right** through the air.
- On landing, it skids and kicks off to the right side.

How to hit it:

- Slightly open your racquet face, using a continental or eastern grip
- Place your shoulders **parallel to the sideline, perpendicular to net.**
- Swing **left to right and slightly forward.**
- Use a **firm wrist** and keep the **non-hitting arm extended** in the opposite direction for balance.

Underspin or Backspin Forehand & Backhand

How to hit it:

- Set up similarly to slice, but: Swing **straight forward**, not across.
- Produces **backward spin**, causing the ball to stay low and skid.
- Avoid slicing across the body—keep the racket path parallel to the sideline and perpendicular to the baseline.

Think: **"Safe" gesture**— arms separating like an umpire signaling a runner is safe in baseball.

Slightly open your racquet face, with a **firm wrist**, and hit **through the ball**. Use **visualization**: close your eyes, picture the flight path and feel of each spin. It helps to reinforce muscle memory.

Footwork: Adjustment Steps

Don't relax on the "easy" ball. That's when footwork matters most.

Small, quick **adjustment steps** help you stay balanced and in position. In French, it's called **"tricotter"** meaning knitting—because of the tiny, rapid movements similar to the needles when knitting 😊.

Especially when:

- The ball comes **straight at you**
- The wind **moves the ball at the last second**
- You're trying to fine-tune your position

Think of your feet as your shot's best friend—**tiny steps lead to big improvements and well executed shots**.

Open Stance vs. Closed Stance

Closed Stance

- Toes point **toward the sideline**
- Shoulders turn **perpendicular to the net**

- More traditional, used often on **backhands** and slower setups

Open Stance

- Toes point more **toward the net & parallel to the baseline**

- Shoulders still turn sideways to create **upper-lower body separation**

- Weight on the **outside leg** (Right hander: right leg for forehand, left for backhand Lefthander: left leg for forehand, right leg for backhand)

- Open stance = faster preparation / longer swing pattern / quicker recovery

That's why it's dominant in today's fast-paced game. Legends like **Serena and Venus Williams** regularly hit open-stance backhands and forehands and most modern players use open stance on forehands as well as on their backhands.

When you're pushed wide or on the run, **open stance saves time** and sets you up to recover quickly.

Sophie Amiach showcases the open-stance forehand

PART II:

Tactics and Tips

Tactics are the heart of match play.

While technique is built on the practice court, tactics should take center stage during competition. Avoid making major technical changes mid-match—they can disrupt your rhythm and confidence. Instead, stick to small corrections using mental cues and shadow strokes. For example, if you miss a serve into the net, simply remind yourself to "reach higher" on the next one. Let your in-match adjustments be guided by smart tactical choices, not mechanical overhauls.

Court Geometry In Action

I grew up playing on red clay and my coach Bernard Paul used to draw court diagrams directly on the surface. He taught me to **use angles and court geometry** to my advantage.

For example: If you're pulled wide behind the baseline and choose to go **down-the-line**, your shot needs **pace, depth and precision**. Otherwise, you'll leave the **crosscourt angle wide open** for your opponent to finish the point. If you can't make the down-the-line shot difficult for your opponent, go **crosscourt deep** or **down-the-middle**, and wait for a better opportunity.

Down-the-line shots are best hit from **inside the baseline**, where your straighter shot path gives your opponent less time to react.

A newer and increasingly popular tactic is the short-angle crosscourt, hit with less pace but sharper angle. This shot pulls your opponent wide off the court, opening up space for a clean winner to the open court or a well-timed tactic "wrong-footing" your opponent by hitting a shot behind them.

But here's the key: when responding to a sharply angled ball, don't move sideways—move toward the bounce and cut the angle. If you shift laterally without cutting in, the ball will keep pulling away from you, and you'll be chasing it instead of intercepting it.

Again, remember the Billie Jean King mantra:

"Cut the angle—run toward the bounce!"

Body Return of Serve

The **body return**—hitting the return directly at your opponent—is now widely used on both the ATP and WTA Tours. It's especially effective because:

- The server is still recovering from their motion and has **little time to react**.
- A shot at the body **removes angles**, making the next shot difficult.

Don't overlook this simple but powerful tactic.

Serve and Volley

Today's game sees less serve-and-volley play, mostly due to:

1. **Discomfort at the net**, particularly with the **transition ball** (the first ball hit after serving).

2. **Lack of explosiveness**—players often arrive too late and face awkward half-volleys.

3. **Slower courts and fluffier balls**, which give **returners more time** to set up.

That said, it can still be a **lethal surprise tactic**, especially if you:

- Hit a **body serve** to jam your opponent.

- Serve with **less pace and more spin** (e.g., kick or slice) to buy yourself some time to get to the net.

- Use it on **game points or pressure moments** (like 40–0 or deuce) for maximum surprise.

Need inspiration? Watch **Martina Navratilova, Stefan Edberg, Billie Jean King, Rod Laver**, or the elegant "ballerina" himself, **Roger Federer**—masters of the transition ball. In today's game watch Novak Djokovic, Jannik Sinner, Carlos Alcaraz, Hailey Baptiste, Aryna Sabalenka or Coco Gauff

A Return of Serve Strategy

Before the serve is hit, **choose your return target**. This keeps you committed and reactive, not indecisive. The **down-the-line return** is especially valuable:

- It's the **furthest point from the server**.
- It takes time away from them.
- It's straight and efficient—just aim **1–2 feet inside** the baseline and sideline for safety.

Another strong return? Right **into the server's body**. It causes:

- **Reaction delays**, especially for taller or slower players.
- Awkward contact from players with **longer preparation motions**.

Similarly, serving **into the returner's body** can limit their options. Observe your opponent's habits. If they stand close or have a slow wind-up, jam them with pace by hitting hard at their body with your serve

Passing Shots

When attempting a **passing shot**, aim for a **landing spot inside the service box**—crosscourt or down-the-line. Why?

- If you hit deeper and your opponent reaches it, they'll volley **above net height**.
- But if you keep it low, they're forced into a difficult **low volley**, which must travel upward—giving you more time to react and unleash your next passing shot.

Move forward into your passing shot. The **extra momentum** adds **pace and height** and helps you **follow through** to the next ball. Ideally, you'll finish **in front of the baseline**, ready to strike again or take the ball in the air or run towards a drop shot volley.

Down-the-Middle Approach

Most players forget the **center of the court** is a fantastic place to aim your approach shot.

Why it works:

1. It **removes angle options** from your opponent's passing shot.
2. It forces them to hit around their body, which is **harder to time and execute**.

This is especially effective against:

- **Tall players**, who struggle to reposition quickly.
- **Slower movers**, who can't get out of the way in time.

- Players with **long swing preparations**, who get jammed and hit late.

Wrong-Footing Your Opponent

When your opponent is recovering from one side and moving laterally, hit **behind them**. Especially if their hips and shoulders are facing the opposite sideline, in that case, they'll struggle to change direction.

Pro tip: Recover by moving with your **outside foot first**—it's faster and covers more ground than crossing over with the inside foot. Always **face the net** during recovery for better balance and options.

Shot Selection

Players come in all shapes, sizes and skill sets. They may vary in athleticism and technique, but the fundamentals of stroke play remain largely the same. That's why *shot selection* is a crucial key to success.

That may sound simple—but in reality, you often have only a split second to decide what shot to hit next. And yet, the best players rarely choose wrong.

Take Chris Evert. She wasn't the most powerful player on tour, but her shot selection was masterful. She had an uncanny ability to put the ball exactly where it was the most uncomfortable for her opponents to hit theirs.

Combine that with her one-of-a-kind mental toughness and she put relentless pressure on opponents—forcing them to go for more and often causing unforced errors.

I played her once. Once. And I felt that pressure firsthand. It wasn't just talent—it was strategy, precision and grit. That's what gave her such remarkable longevity and consistent success.

Another brilliant on-court mind? Agnieszka (Aga) Radwanska. She didn't rely on power either, but her tactical thinking and shot selection were exceptional. With placement, angles, and impeccable timing, she carved out an extraordinary career—outsmarting opponents and painting the court like a true artist with the racket.

Anticipation

Speaking of Radwanska, this section belongs to her.

You've probably heard commentators say, *"She anticipates so well—it's like she knows where the ball's going before her opponent even hits it."* And it's true—it can feel that way. But no, Radwanska's not reading minds. What she *is* reading is body language, racket angle and position before her opponents stroke their shots, giving subtle cues before the moment of contact.

Aga was a master of this instinctual foresight. Can it be taught? To a degree. You can study an opponent's patterns, observe their habits, and train yourself to read the angle of their racket before they make contact. But true anticipation—*elite* anticipation—often comes down to feel. Some players just have it.

Still, if you watch enough film, study your opponents, and play with intent, you *can* sharpen this skill. You may not become Radwanska overnight—but you'll start reading the court like a seasoned pro.

The Slice Serve – Short and Wide

For right-handers (opposite for lefties), a well-placed slice serve on the deuce side (right side when facing the net) can be a game-changer. But here's the catch: it needs to land *short* in the service box—not deep. Why? Because a short slice pushes your opponent *wide* off the court, forcing them into a desperate diagonal run just to reach it.

Most returners instinctively move sideways along the baseline, but slice makes the ball curve away after the bounce. The result? They're left scrambling and stretched, often unable to hit a solid return. In contrast, a deep slice gives your opponent time, space, and better positioning—basically handing them a return they can work with.

So where should you aim? For right-handers: keep your slice short in the service box and toward the sideline. For lefties, the same principle applies—especially on the ad side. And here's the kicker: lefties get even more mileage out of this serve. Oh yes, they do!

Why Do Left-Handed Players Have An Advantage?

Left-handers in tennis enjoy a real edge—and that's no myth.

When tennis rules were created, wooden racquets, low-power games and limited amount of spin were the norm. But today's game is a different beast: carbon fiber racquets, explosive strength, lightning-fast serves, wicked spin. And yet, the scoring system hasn't evolved to match this modern era.

So why do lefties still dominate key moments?

It comes down to the advantage (Ad) side of the court—where the most critical points in a game are played **AKA the GAME POINTS:**

40–0 40–30 All Advantage points

Three of the four crucial game points are played from the ad side—and for left-handers, that's their natural side to serve from with that signature slicing spin. On the biggest points of the game, they're hitting their most dangerous serve—pulling players and especially right-handers far off the court and opening up the entire playing field.

It's not just an advantage—it's a literal one.

A well-placed lefty slice serve can yank an opponent deep into the double's alley, leaving the rest of the court wide open for an easy put-away… if the return comes back at all.

Only one game point truly favors right-handed players at 40-15 –when they can use their slice serve to an equal advantage. Just one out of four! 1 out of 4 really!

Deuce Side vs. Advantage Side

How do we address the natural edge that left-handed players enjoy—an edge that didn't fully surface until the game evolved, especially around the time of "Rocket" Rod Laver? Laver's devastating slice serve became a serious weapon against players especially right-handers—and remember, he was doing it with a wooden racquet and on the fastest surface played on at the time: grass. Imagine the damage he could do with today's technology!

Since then, legends like John McEnroe, Jimmy Connors, Martina Navratilova, Monica Seles, Petra Kvitová, Rafael Nadal (and many more) have benefited from the same edge. It's remarkable, really—lefties make up a small percentage of players, yet a surprisingly large number have reached world No. 1 and won multiple major titles. Just look at this list of left-handers who topped the rankings: Rod Laver, Jimmy Connors, John McEnroe, Thomas Muster, Marcelo Ríos, Rafael Nadal, Martina Navratilova, Monica Seles and Angelique Kerber. Coincidence? I think not.

So, How Could We Level The Playing Field?

Simple. When a right-hander plays a lefty, the right-handed player should serve first *from the ad side* (at 0–0). That way, they get to serve three of the four key points of a game from their stronger **deuce** side—mirroring the natural pattern that favors lefties. Or flip it: have the lefty start serving on the **deuce side**, where their slice serve won't dominate the biggest points. Voilà—a more balanced match.

(And in case you're wondering—I'm right-handed, and I had the privilege of playing Martina Navratilova at Wimbledon in 1990. Her lefty slice serve? Absolutely spectacular. She went on to win the title that year—her 18th and final major singles crown. Martina, I was happy to do my part! 😊

Left-handed Player's Advantage

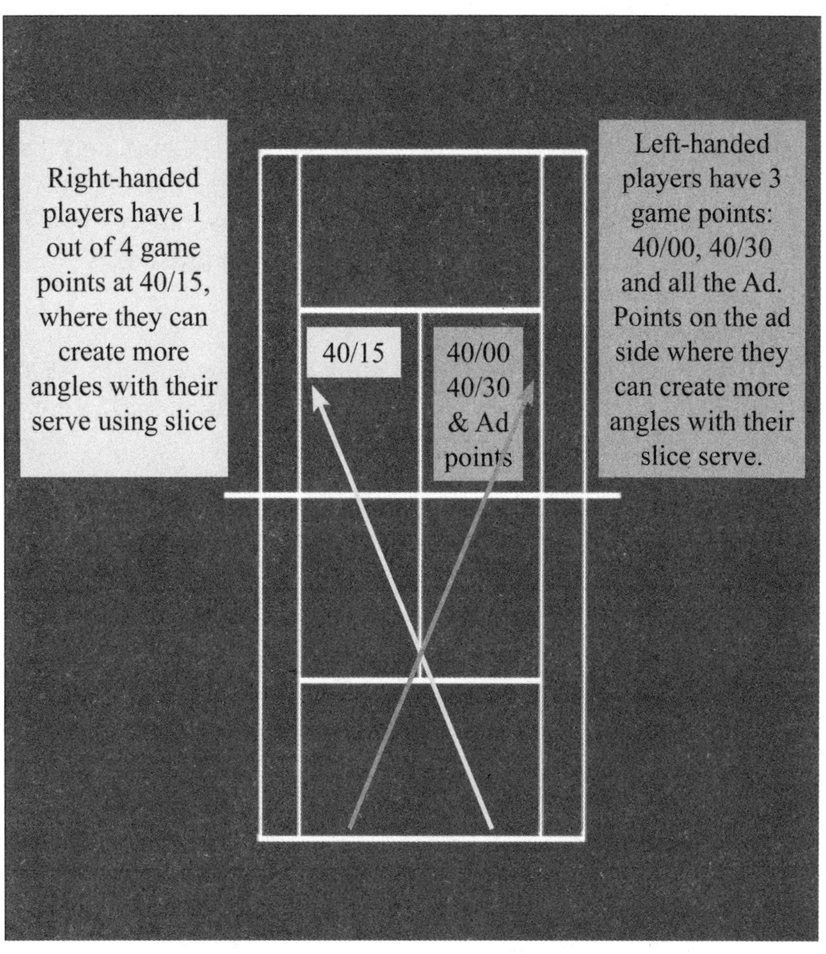

Mirroring Techniques

One of the best ways to improve your game? Practice in front of a mirror. Watch your footwork. Rehearse your strokes. Get into rhythm.

Barbara Potter, one of the best serve-and-volley players of my era, used this method often. I remember seeing her in the gym before matches, practicing to music—completely in the zone, studying her own form. She looked like she was having fun, and that joy translated to her game. She became a US Open semifinalist and a Top 10 player in both singles (No. 7) and doubles (No. 3).

Did I mention she was left-handed? 😊

Her adjustment steps were some of the best on tour. And I truly believe her mirror workouts were a major part of her success. Try it for yourself—it's productive *and* fun, especially if you're into music and movement.

The Inside-Out & Inside-In Forehands

These shots, used by amateurs and pros alike—both rely on one thing: **quick footwork**.

The inside-out forehand is hit when you run around your backhand and drive the ball diagonally across the court. The inside-in forehand is also hit by running around your backhand, but instead, you drive the ball straight down the line. Both are powerful weapons because it's hard for your opponent to read your intent—your shoulder turn hides your direction until the last moment.

The key difference? For the inside-in, you make contact slightly farther in front of your body. For the inside-out, just a touch later. Your racket head and follow-through take care of the rest, guiding the ball where it needs to go.

So why is footwork so important? Because you need to circle around the ball and create enough space to swing freely.

Get too close, and you'll end up jammed—leaving the opposite side of the court wide open for your opponent to counter.

Watch Steffi Graf. Her inside-out forehand is legendary. She moved like she had springs in her shoes, always getting into perfect position. Her husband, Andre Agassi, was just as brilliant with this shot. Honestly, they may have had the best forehand footwork of their eras. And if their kids ever did pick up a racket—watch out!

Footwork - The Vertical Push

Have you ever noticed how top players seem to lift off the ground at the moment of impact? That's called the vertical push—and it's a vital tool, especially for shorter players. I first was made aware of that technique by Thierry Champion, a former Top 50 ATP player and two-time major quarterfinalist. The vertical push allows players to strike the ball at a higher contact point, giving them more control and a better angle over the net. Jasmine Paolini is a great example of someone who uses this technique beautifully.

Watch slow-motion footage of players like Carlos Alcaraz or Ons Jabeur, and you'll see it in action—sometimes both feet are completely off the ground during their groundstrokes. It's especially striking on those "jumping backhands" from Jannik Sinner or Paolini. It's not just beautiful to watch—it's a serious weapon in play.

Chasing A Lob

You've been lobbed. You're sprinting back. Don't run directly under the ball—that's a common mistake. It often leads to getting jammed after the bounce or, worse, getting hit by the ball off your back as you are running.

The trick? Run *alongside* the ball. Get ahead of it. This gives you room to rotate and choose your shot—whether you choose to hit a regular groundstroke, a lob or a passing shot if your opponent followed their lob to the net. If that is the case, consider hitting a lob to their backhand side after chasing their own lob. It's a much tougher shot for them to volley and they might have to chase your lob if it is hit with depth and accuracy. If they stay back, go on offense. Just make your decision *early* and commit as you chase down their lob.

Drill: Hit the wall. Use a wall. Hit overheads so the ball bounces off the ground and rebounds high above your head, simulating a lob. Then practice turning and hitting your shot.

The Wall Is The Perfect Practice Partner

Walls and backboards are tennis treasures. Sadly, many clubs have removed them—but they're one of the best tools you'll ever find. Why? Because the wall never misses. Hit it hard, it comes back harder.

You learn control—or the ball teaches you. Aryna Sabalenka had to learn to tame her power. Lindsay Davenport too. Whether or not they used a wall, they *understood* that power means nothing without control. Most pros will tell you; they trained against a wall. So, did I. I used to play in the garage of my apartment complex in France.

On rainy days, I'd rig the light timer with a matchstick and hit for hours—just me and the wall. When I was four, no one would play with me. So, I made up games. I'd draw circles on the wall and challenge myself to hit alternating forehands and backhands 20 times in a row. If I succeeded? I'd "beat the wall." My parents humored me—but hey, it worked!

Make up your own rules. Be creative. Grab your racket and go beat the wall. 😊

Sophie Amiach showcases a one-handed backhand on the backboard

Sophie Amiach, on two different occasions, with fellow broadcaster and Hall of Famer Mary Carillo

PART III:

Common Mistakes & Uncommon Good Fixes

The best way to correct a mistake quickly is to look at the end result. In other words—how and where did you miss your shot?

If you felt late on the ball, the issue was likely your footwork or body positioning at impact. To improve this, exaggerate your small, quick adjustment steps as you prepare to hit. If you listen closely during a live match—or even while watching on TV—you'll often hear players' shoes squeaking, especially on hard courts. The better the player, the more squeaking you'll hear. That's great footwork in action.

Billie Jean King often compared tennis movement to ballet: upper body straight, strong posture, quick and balanced footwork. Think of those small, precise adjustment steps as part of a dance. Rhythm matters too—so go ahead, turn up the music and start moving!

One of the best examples? Monsieur Federer, of course. He seemed to glide effortlessly across the court, his footwork and balance a thing of beauty. On the women's side, Sloane Stephens comes to mind—her movement is just as graceful and efficient.

Now, what if you didn't feel late and your positioning felt solid—but you still missed the shot? That's when you ask yourself a few quick questions:

- Where did the ball land?
- Did it hit the bottom of the net? Just clip the top? Go too long or fall too short?

Once you've identified the outcome, backtrack. Try to recall how the shot felt. Where was your point of contact?

Billie Jean King emphasizes this fundamental truth: it's all about point of contact. If you hit the ball in the right spot—even if your footwork wasn't perfect—you'll still make a decent shot. For most strokes, that point of contact should be in front of your body.

There are exceptions, of course. Kick serves and shots like inside-out forehands and backhands in doubles often requires contacting the ball slightly less in front to create the desire angle.

A great example: Natasha Zvereva's return game in the 1980s. Especially in doubles, from the deuce side, she'd contact the ball a bit later and create sharp angles with her two-handed backhand—sometimes putting her own partner at risk at the net with how sharp those returns were! Sabalenka is also a master at it especially off of her backhand return from the deuce side

Keep practicing this habit of backtracking. At first, it may take time, but soon you'll be reading your mistakes like a computer—spotting patterns and fixing issues on the fly.

One last reminder: don't overanalyze during a match. Nothing disrupts your rhythm faster. And remember, you only get 20 to 25 seconds between points. Save deep technical corrections for the practice court.

Improving technique is hard work—and for professionals on the WTA and ATP Tours, the off-season is usually the best time to do it. The problem? The off-season is very short.

Sometimes I wonder if players should consider taking more time off, skipping a few months of the tour to really perfect their game. It's not an easy decision, but it can be necessary to become your best possible self. Most pros make changes and immediately rejoin the tour after their brief off-season, leaving little time for new techniques to fully take hold. Take Novak Djokovic, for example, when he changed his serve technique. Sabalenka and Iga Swiatek also overhauled their serve and toss. I've often thought Coco Gauff could benefit from a three-month hiatus to shift her forehand grip away from an extreme western grip and refine her upper body mechanics on her serve. If you're an amateur, it might be worth stepping away from match play for a few weeks—or even a few months—to focus purely on technical adjustments. That's when you'll see real gains.

But during a tournament or match? Keep it simple. Focus on small cues and quick corrections. In match play, your priority should always be tactics.

A Few Solutions To Universal Problems

Groundstrokes Landing at the Bottom of the Net

Are you closing the face of your racket at impact and hitting the ball down? Keep your racket face as parallel to the ball as possible through impact. Use top spin to create more arch for better net clearance.

Right-handed Player vs. Left-Handed Opponent

There are a few adjustments to be made when playing a left-handed player. First, always try practicing or warming up with a left-handed player ahead of your match. Then during your match, remember most left-handed players use a slice serve that will travel to your left after landing, so move your initial return position one foot to your left from your normal position when playing a left-handed player, opposites applies for left-handed players playing against a right-handed player.

Facing Heavy Topspin Groundstrokes

In this case, there are two solutions.

First option: Move up onto—or just inside—the baseline to meet your opponent's heavy topspin shot early. By taking the ball closer to the bounce, you avoid letting the spin jump up above shoulder height, where it becomes much harder to control. This early positioning gives you a cleaner strike zone and keeps you in an offensive mindset.

From here, you can hit a regular backhand, or, if you're comfortable, use your backhand slice/underspin. And if you're not? Well, it's time to work on it! While you're at it, add a forehand slice/underspin to your toolkit too. Both are useful weapons against high-bouncing topspin. Slicing/Underspin are all about timing, so practice regularly with your coach or hitting partner using drills that simulate those high, loopy balls. The more reps you get, the more natural you will feel under pressure.

You can also choose to hit a flat forehand or backhand. The key here is to keep your racquet head level with the ball at contact—especially since that contact will likely be around shoulder height. Avoid swinging down into the ball, which often sends it straight into the net. Instead, think about hitting through the ball, keeping your racquet on-plane and accelerating with a controlled finish.

Second option: Take a few steps back behind the baseline. This gives the ball time to drop to a more manageable height after the bounce, letting you hit it with a standard forehand, backhand slice, flat stroke, or topspin. Just remember—once you've hit the shot, recover forward toward the baseline. Backing up opens the court and makes you vulnerable to a drop shot or short ball, so don't stay too deep for too long. This deeper positioning also requires more physical effort. You'll need strong footwork and extra energy to move, adjust, and re-set for each shot—but it can be an effective strategy when used wisely.

Competing Against A Player Who Has A Wicked Slice or Underspin Forehand and/or Backhand

Underspin, as mentioned earlier, causes the ball to stay low and skid after the bounce—faster on grass and hard courts, and a bit slower on clay but still very difficult to play. It's essential to adjust your footwork depending on the surface and be ready to move up quickly. Think of how a ball skips when it hits a painted line—that's the kind of sudden skid you're dealing with.

Once you've moved into position, the key is to **get your racquet head below the level of the ball**. To do this, relax your wrist downward so the racquet naturally drops beneath the ball. From there, **accelerate with a strong low-to-high and forward motion** to generate topspin. This fast upward swing helps neutralize the skidding effect of underspin.

It's not so much a forward-driving motion as it is a high-energy, upward lift—one that creates spin, arc, and net clearance, giving you valuable margin for error. Think: spin over speed, lift over drive.

This technique also applies when facing a slower underspin. Even if the ball doesn't skid aggressively, you still need to counter its reverse rotation. Stay alert: slices can curve sideways after bouncing, so be ready to **move toward the ball** and adjust your spacing. Always aim to strike early and stay balanced.

But what if the ball stays too low to get your racquet underneath it—especially if you use a pronounced western grip? That's when it's time to fight slice with slice. A solid backhand or forehand slice of your own can be the perfect response. To do that effectively, you may need to shift from your western grip to something more neutral or even a continental grip. Coco Gauff is absolutely brilliant at it.

If your opponent frequently uses slice as their main groundstroke, having your own slice in your toolkit becomes essential. It's not just a defensive shot—it's a way to stay in rallies, change pace and respond with precision.

My suggestion? Head back to the practice court with your coach or teaching professional and spend dedicated time learning to both **handle** and **hit** slice and underspin. You'll gain confidence, variety, and one more way to take control of the point.

Groundstrokes Hitting the Top of the Net

Add more top spin (low-to-high and forward motion) especially if you are going down-the-line over the highest part of the net.

Groundstrokes Wide or Long

If you're missing wide or long, it's time to give yourself more margin for error. Instead of aiming directly at the lines, aim at least a foot inside the court. If you're still missing, increase that margin even more. For balls that are hit long adjust also with more top spin.

In the worst-case scenario, reset your rhythm by hitting safely down the middle of the court a few times. This helps you regain feel, confidence, and control before attempting riskier shots near the lines again.

Another factor to consider is your racket setup. Switching to a tighter string pattern can help with control. The tighter the strings, the less movement—and therefore, the less "trampoline effect"—as the ball leaves your racquet. This reduces launch and helps keep your shots in play with more control.

That's why you'll often see professional players switching to freshly strung racquets during ball changes in a match. New balls fly faster through the air, so players compensate by using tighter strings to maintain control.

The same principle applies when playing in high-altitude locations like Madrid or Bogotá—or in dry, thin air environments like Indian Wells, California. The ball travels faster and farther in these conditions, so a tighter string pattern can make a noticeable difference in keeping your shots within the lines. Of course, there are exceptions—like Adrian Mannarino who strings his racquets as low as 19-25 lbs. (8.6-11 kg) regardless of the weather conditions or surface. He's truly one of a kind. Most players are stringing at 45-55 lbs. (20-25 kg)

Serve Lands at the Bottom of the Net

Is your upper body collapsing at contact? Chances are, yes. Many players tend to bend forward at impact—especially when reaching for the ball. Instead, focus on keeping your upper body upright and your head stable as you hit. Think about maintaining length through your spine and feel a stretch through your rib cage as you make contact. That extension adds both power and control.

Serve Goes Long or Wide

Once again—give yourself more margin for error. Don't aim for the line; aim at least a foot inside the court. Precision improves with confidence, and confidence builds from consistency. So, play the smart percentages.

Also, don't hesitate to mix things up and occasionally fire a serve down the middle of the box—right into your opponent's body. It's uncomfortable to return and highly effective, especially under pressure.

If your serve is sailing long, check your point of contact. Chances are, you're either hitting the ball behind you, contacting it with an open racquet face, or striking too low and too far in front. If that's the case, revisit your toss and adjust it to the optimal zone.

Another issue could be that you're hitting the ball too flat. Add more topspin. The more rotation and movement your serve has through the air, the "heavier" the ball becomes—and the more gravity will help pull it down into the box.

Second Serves Into The Net (aka Double Faults)

When your second serve is crashing into the net—or worse, you're racking up double faults—the first thing to do is add spin. Whether you're using a kick or slice serve, accelerate your racquet head through the point of contact to generate more spin.

Here's a mental mantra that can help. Go slow at the start of your motion, then fast once the racket is behind your back accelerating through impact. This rhythm helps create fluidity and power in your serve motion.

If nerves creep in or you've missed several in a row, dial it back. Hit at half your usual pace, but with extra spin—until you're landing the serve consistently. Don't worry about pace until you've rebuilt your rhythm.

Drop Shot Into The Net

If your drop shot keeps catching the net, check your wrist. Keep it firm at impact—**no scooping**. Trying to "guide" the ball often leads to a swing that's too short and underpowered. A firm, confident motion, with good feel, gives the ball enough lift to clear the net while keeping it short.

Drop Shot Too High or Deep

You may be opening your racquet face too much by scooping under the ball. That creates excessive height and depth. Shorten your follow-through just enough to control the distance—but not so much that the ball dies in the net. It's a fine balance. Keep the motion compact, the wrist firm and steady.

Volleys Into The Net

Important: Block your wrist at impact. If the volley you hit is below the level of the net, slightly open the face of the racket and hit with a firm wrist.

If the ball is higher than the level of the net, keep your wrist firm and make sure your arm is above or level with the net at impact. Do not allow your arm to drop below the level of the net, as this will bring the ball down with it.

If you hit a swing volley, avoid hitting the top of the ball with your racket head. Remember to drop your wrist below the level of the ball and create top spin with a fast low-to-high motion.

Volleys Hit Long

Make sure your racket face is not open, and your point of contact is in front of you. A classic volley is short and compact, so avoid taking too large a swing at the ball. When hitting a swing volley, make sure your wrist remains below the level of the ball before impact, and create lots of top spin hitting with a fast low-to-high motion. The more spin you create, the safer your swing volley will be, since velocity and heaviness will land faster within the limits of the court due to gravity.

Underspin Shots Hit In The Net Or Too Deep Into the net.

When standing at the baseline, keep your racket level with the ball and swing through the ball in a straight-line pattern. If your motion moves too far downwards (especially from a deep position in the court), chances are you will encounter the net. Hitting with a slice (or underspin) on a low ball, slightly open your racket face while hitting through the ball extending your arm towards your target at impact.

Too deep. The only time you really need a high-to-low motion is when you're hitting a high ball—meaning one that bounces above net level, usually landing on or inside the service line. In these situations, use a slight high-to-low, downward motion to help keep the ball from flying long.

That said, I've seen Ben Shelton hit forehands from the baseline off balls above his head using a subtle high-to-low and forward motion. He's a master at it. It's a tough shot to pull off unless you're tall. While Shelton isn't the tallest player out there, he generates incredible pace thanks to his upper body strength. Given the height and speed of the incoming ball, that slight high-to-low and forward motion becomes essential to keep the ball in play and avoid overshooting.

Still struggling with shots going too deep? A few possible culprits: your racket might be too open at contact, or your grip may not be firm enough during the strike. Both can cause the ball to float and carry farther than you want.

Slice Shots Hit In The Net Or Too Deep

If your slice backhand or forehand is landing in the net or sailing too deep, here's what to check. Just like I mentioned earlier, make sure your racket head isn't moving downward at the moment of contact—otherwise, the ball will likely drop into the net. On the other hand, if your slice is flying long, focus on keeping your racket face from opening up at impact. A firm wrist throughout the shot is key to staying in control and keeping the ball low and precise.

PART IV:

Mind Matters - Mental Toughness

A quote from Billie Jean King perfectly sums up this chapter: **"Pressure is a privilege and champions adjust."**

Just like in life, tennis demands constant adjustment. And often, the player who adapts fastest is the one who wins. One of the most powerful tools for success on the court is mental toughness—the ability to stay composed, resilient and focused, no matter what the situation.

Expect the Unexpected

Preparation goes far beyond physical training. True success comes from minimizing surprises. Cross every "t," dot every "i." Before a match, visualize worst-case scenarios. Picture tricky conditions—wind, sun glare, bad lighting, questionable line calls, unfamiliar balls. Then, train under those same conditions. Ask your hitting partner to make bad calls. Play in the heat. My friend and great lead commentator Pete Odgers also advises to practice delay of play, like a rain delays. He is not wrong. Practice when you're tired or frustrated. Learn to be comfortable being uncomfortable.

Some things will always be out of your control. That's exactly when your mental game matters most.

Training Your Mind

Yes, your mind can be trained—just like your body. There are books, podcasts and exercises dedicated entirely to building mental toughness. The way you think directly affects how you perform. Emotional strength is every bit as important as physical conditioning.

A core skill is **positive self-talk**. Frame your thoughts in a way that builds you up. Instead of saying, "I always hit my forehand into the net," say, "I will add more topspin to clear the net." Instead of, "I'm always late to the ball," say, "I will react faster and hit earlier." Your inner voice should sound like your biggest fan—not your harshest critic.

Another powerful tool is **visualization**. Close your eyes and imagine executing your shots perfectly. See the ball clearing the net, landing deep in the court, your footwork crisp and confident. Replay that mental movie often. Your brain doesn't know the difference between real and imagined success—so keep imagining it until it feels real. And finally, **carry yourself with confidence**. Shoulders back, head up. Walk like you belong out there—because you do. It signals strength to your opponent and, more importantly, to yourself. Whether you're up or down in the score, you want to look as if you're winning. Own your presence and win the game.

Focus On What You Can Control

You can control:

- Your coach and team

- Your technique

- Your equipment
- Tactical knowledge
- Fitness and recovery
- Nutrition
- Travel plans
- Mental routines and rituals

Focus only on what you can influence. Let go of the rest. The less stress, the better your performance.

Practice Positivity

Practice being positive off the court too. Surround yourself with people who lift you up. Positivity is contagious. Challenges will come—don't run from them. Embrace them. Each tough moment is a lesson in resilience.

Sleep, Nutrition and Travel

- **Sleep**: Prioritize it. Experiment with what helps you rest—meditation, music, yoga. Bring your own pillow if it helps!

- **Nutrition**: Learn what fuels *your* body best. What works for others may not work for you. Test and refine your meals before, during, and after matches.

- **Travel**: Arrive early to adjust to jet lag and new environments. Stretch and move during and after long car or plane rides.

Surface, Conditions and Equipment

Try to warm up on your tournament court. Every court plays differently—even if the dimensions are the same. Faster courts, slower courts, indoor lighting, wind, heat—it all matters.

Take time to:

- Adjust to the speed of the surface.
- Prepare earlier if the ball is coming faster.
- Back up on volleys and returns if your opponent hits big.

Check your racket, strings and grips. Bring at least two or more rackets—ideally with different string tensions. And always practice with the tournament balls if possible.

Recover Right

Recovery is a science. Stretch after every match. Learn what recovery methods work best for you—massage, ice bath, stretching, rest. Even short matches require proper recovery.

Enjoy The Game

You play your best when you're having fun. Stay present. Embrace the joy of the moment. HAVE FUN!

PART V:

More Tips For Better Play

Butterflies

I've never met a player—pro or amateur—who didn't feel at least a little nervous before stepping onto the court. And you know what? That's a good thing. It means you care. Learning how to manage those butterflies will help you settle in faster and perform your best. Here are a few pre-match tricks to help calm the nerves:

- Create a warm-up routine that keeps your mind off the match. Work up a good sweat. Listen to music. Dance a little. Dance a lot—why not?

- Shake out your arms and legs to get your blood flowing. (Check out Jannik Sinner's pre-match ball drills—they're innovative and fun.)

- Close your eyes. Take a few deep breaths. Picture something relaxing. My go-to? Floating in the ocean with the warm sun on my skin.

- During warm-up, exaggerate your footwork with small, quick adjustment steps. Stay light on your feet between points. Staying physically active helps burn off nervous energy.

- Go into the match with a clear game plan. Focus on execution: "Where will I serve?" "Where will I return?" Stick to short, simple thoughts—one shot, one point at a time. Billie Jean King would often say, "One ball at a time."

- Don't peek at the score. Stay in the present moment as it would distract you from the task at hand.

- Stay positive. Visualize success.

These tips help bring your focus to the present moment, where your best tennis lives.

Rituals

We all have little rituals that center us. But under pressure, they're often the first things to slip. Know yours, practice them and rely on them—especially in tight moments.

Whether it's how many times you bounce the ball before a serve, how you adjust your strings, or where you stand to return, your rituals can ground you. They offer a sense of control. Stick to what works for you—don't just copy other players. Their rituals might throw off your rhythm.

Never Change A Winning Tactic

You've heard it before: "If it ain't broke, don't fix it." If something's working—even if it feels a little boring—don't abandon it. How many times have you switched tactics too early, only to find yourself in a third-set scramble? Stick with what's working. Keep it simple.

Always Have A Plan B (And C)

When your main strategy isn't working, it's time to pivot. Down 0–3? 0–4? That's your cue. Don't keep doing what's failing—try something new.

Take Aryna Sabalenka, for example. In Rome 2024, she faced match points against Elina Svitolina. Her signature power game wasn't enough. So she changed it up—introducing a drop shot she rarely used. It flipped the momentum. She not only won, she enjoyed the match. That drop shot has since become a major part of her game. **Adaptability isn't just useful—it's essential.**

Keeping Track

Your strengths are the shots you trust under pressure. Your weaknesses? Usually, the ones that crumble when it counts.

Keep track—of your opponents and yourself. Watch how they play. Take notes after matches: favorite shots, tendencies, patterns. Did they keep hitting that forehand down the line for a winner? Next time, don't give them that chance. Also track yourself. What worked? What didn't? What helped you bounce back? Build a "tennis library" with insights about your own game. If possible, review match footage. Share it with your coach. The more you know, the fewer surprises during match time.

Got a match coming up? Revisit those notes. Professionals often pull out their match notes on changeovers—it's not a grocery list; it's a game plan.

Facing an Unknown Opponent

No data? No problem. Ask around—friends, coaches, fellow players. Watch their practice. Scout warm-ups. Look online for videos or match stats.

In the warm-up, gather intel: Are they right- or left-handed? How's their technique? Comfortable at the net? Agile? Watch closely. Every clue helps.

Changeovers

Use this time to reset. Think about what just happened and what you can adjust.

- Hydrate—before you're thirsty. Dehydration can sneak up.
- Breathe—deep, slow breaths lower your heart rate.
- Refuel with a snack or energy drink if needed.
- Recenter—use visualization or affirmations to calm your mind.

Don't waste these moments. They're golden.

After A Long Rally

Both you and your opponent are tired. Use that to your advantage.

- Focus on making your next first serve—don't risk a double fault.

- Serve to the middle of the service box for higher margin.
- Use your legs to compensate for fatigue.
- If you're returning, get the ball in play still being aggressive but give yourself a big target and margin for error, hit a down the middle return. Go for high-percentage shots.

If your opponent looks spent, keep the pressure on—especially if you're serving. **They have to match your pace.**

Playing An Injured Opponent

This is a mental test. Some players are hurt. Some are acting. Doesn't matter—focus on your game. Don't get distracted. Stick to your strategy, but test them: a drop shot, a side-to-side rally. Keep your cool. Control what's on your side of the net.

Take Your Time

There's no need to rush. Most players speed up when they're close to the finish line. Don't fall into that trap.

Take your time between points. Stick to your rituals. The match ends when it ends—don't force it.

Visualization = Manifestation

The top athletes use it all the time. Bianca Andreescu visualized winning the US Open before it happened. She even wrote herself a fake check as a teen. Her mind led the way before her body followed.

Having trouble with your serve? Close your eyes. Picture the perfect toss, the smooth motion, the ball landing just inside the box where you are aiming.

The brain responds to visualization like it's an actual practice. Use it to fine-tune any part of your game.

Watch matches—attend tournaments as an amateur, track players with styles similar to yours. You'll pick up tactics and rhythm just by observing. And yes, even watching from your couch can help. As for you pros, pick a player per tournament and go watch them, take notes that you can add to your computer library. Build up that library and the next time you face that player you can pull all the information necessary for you to have an edge from the start.

Meditation

Meditation helps you stay grounded. Try it. Reflect, breathe, visualize.

Whatever form works for you—guided meditation, breathing exercises, mindfulness—use it. It's powerful on and off the court.

Practice With Purpose

Repetition only helps if you're reinforcing the right things. Too many players spend hours with a ball machine, practicing the wrong technique over and over—actually harming their game instead of helping it.

If you can, invest in a few private lessons. Learn proper technique, take notes, and then practice with intention.

Watch how the pros train. For them, practice isn't just about hitting balls—it's about footwork, shot selection, movement, and mental toughness.

If you're serious about improving, dedicate 30–50% of your court time to focused practice—not just playing matches. Pros constantly reinforce the basics. That's why even their off days still look solid.

Want to build consistency? Try the two-against-one drill: two players on one side, one on the other. Rotate roles. Switch formations—baseline rallies, volleys, mixed play. It's exhausting, but it sharpens stamina, decision-making, and awareness.

Simulate pressure. Start games at deuce. Use only second serves. Serve and volley once per game. Create your own rules. Reward yourself when you rise to the challenge.

Practice playing 3-out-of-5 tie break matches to get tie break ready when that situation arises in a match.

Get creative. Invent drills. Make it fun. Practice isn't punishment—it's where progress lives.

Ivan Lendl with Sophie Amiach

PART VI:

Does Tennis Need A Few New Rules?

Let's start with the men's game—where most of the adjustments are needed.

One of my biggest pet peeves? Watching very tall players dominate simply because of their serve. When 80% of a player's game is based on aces, something feels off. As much as I respect athletes like John Isner, Ivo Karlovic and Reilly Opelka, their height gives them an outsized advantage.

Over the years, the average height in men's tennis has steadily increased—but the rules haven't. Maybe it's time they did.

Raise The Net...Seriously!

A slightly higher net in the men's game would do more than just disrupt the reign of giant servers. It would lengthen the flight time of both serves and groundstrokes. That gives players more time to react, approach the net, and try serve-and-volley tactics again.

Passing shots would need more height and arc, giving volleyers a real chance to cut them off. That alone could breathe life back into a variety of playing styles—styles that have been buried under a tidal wave of modern technology: faster rackets, more powerful strings, heavier topspin, slower courts.

Despite all this evolution, the rules have barely budged. And that's wild.

Remember the magic of contrast—Borg vs. McEnroe, Navratilova vs. Evert? We've lost that. Today, serve-and-volley tennis is nearly extinct. With slower courts and explosive baseline power, attackers are often forced to volley ankle-high from no-man's-land, only to be passed with ease.

The game has moved on. But the rules haven't.

Another Idea: One Serve Per Point

What if men were allowed only *one* serve per point?

Suddenly, every point becomes a mental game. Do you go for the big serve or play it safe with more spin? The receiver can't anticipate. That unpredictability would add suspense for fans and strategic tension for players. It would also reduce the premium placed on sheer serving power.

Bottom line: If tennis wants to evolve, it shouldn't' just react to new technologies—it should be willing to rethink the rules that shape the sport itself. We don't need a revolution. Just a few bold tweaks.

A New Format For Majors For Both Genders

The best-of-five format in men's tennis is one of the sport's most fiercely defended traditions. But maybe it's time for a smarter, hybrid solution—one that satisfies players, fans, broadcasters and yes, sponsors (who help keep the sport alive).

A Smarter Best-of-Five Format

Here's my proposal:

If a player wins fewer than four games in each of the first two sets—say, 6–2, 6–1—they lose in straight sets. The match ends as a best-of-three. Why give a clearly overmatched player a full five-set window? But if either player wins four or more games per set—6–4, 7—5 then it becomes a full best-of-five. Competitive matches get the time they deserve. Lopsided ones don't drag on needlessly. Yes, the purists will point to historic comebacks—and they're not wrong. But those are rare. Meanwhile, endless, uncompetitive five-setters are all too common. This hybrid format would keep fans engaged, streamline broadcast planning, and better protect players' bodies. Tennis is a year-round grind, and the injury toll is real. If we want stars to stick around longer, we need to take care of them. I would add that all quarterfinals, semifinals and finals men and women would play three-out-of-five sets regardless of the first two sets scores.

No Ad Scoring

I mentioned that for the sake of the new generations, tennis matches have to be shorter and the no-ad scoring will certainly help reduce the length of sometimes endless games. At 40-all or deuce the player who wins the next point will win the game. The receiver will have the choice of what side they would rather return from. This format is already used in doubles in most tournaments let's apply it in singles as well. And by the way that would take one of the three-game points advantage for the lefties away. Trust me if the score reached 40-all, no right-hander in their right mind would have picked the ad side to receive Martina Navratilova's lefty serve!

The Let Serve Debate

Should we play let serves? College tennis does as well as other competitions. Pro tours don't. And personally? I'm not in favor.

No two nets are exactly the same. Tension and post stability vary and that affects how a let ball reacts. Imagine losing match point at Wimbledon on a fluke let-ace off a loose net? No thanks.

Martina Navratilova and I disagree here—she believes it speeds up the game. Billie Jean King has a valid counterpoint: if we play let balls during points, why not on the serve? I hear her. But for me, the drawbacks outweigh the benefits.

One Toss, One Serve

Here's another pet peeve: players tossing the ball, not liking it and starting over. It happens often—especially on the women's tour. Venus Williams, Maria Sharapova and Caroline Garcia, to name a few.

My take? Once the toss is up, you hit it. The toss is part of the motion. Only exception: extreme wind and even then, just one redo. Define it. Regulate it.

Add A Clock Between Serves

Absolutely. Ten seconds between first and second serves. It's enough.

Let's Stop Calling Every Major A "Grand Slam"

This one's about language—and respect. Each of the four events—Australian Open, Roland-Garros, Wimbledon, and the US Open—is a major. A Grand Slam is the achievement of winning all four in a calendar year. Only a handful of players have ever done it:

Men: Don Budge (1938), Rod Laver (1962 & 1969)

Women: Maureen Connolly (1953), Margaret Court (1970), Steffi Graf (1988)

Graf, notably, also won Olympic gold that same year—earning the Golden Slam. That's the level of greatness we're talking about.

So let's be precise: someone who wins one major is a major champion—not a "Grand Slam Champion."

For the trivia lovers: "Grand Slam" came from a 19th-century card game called Boston (a cousin of bridge), where taking all 13 tricks was called—yes—a grand slam. Sportswriters like Alan Gould and John Kieran borrowed it. The rest is history.

Ditch The Pre-Match Warm-Up

The five-minute on-court warm-up? Outdated. Players are already warm from the practice courts. Let them walk on, get the rules, flip the coin and start.

Bathroom Breaks

My friend and fellow commentator Pete Ogers makes a great point: if a set lasts less than 45 minutes, no bathroom break—unless it's a real emergency.

Quick sets followed by long breaks kill momentum and frustrate fans. It's bad for TV, worse for in-person energy.

Towels

I thought COVID had ended the towel ritual—ball kids handling players' sweat. Nope. It's back. And honestly? It's gross. Players can handle their own towels.

Bring Back Line Judges And Challenges

I miss the line crew. And the drama of challenge calls. Remember the hush before a big screen review? That tension was part of the theater. I'm still skeptical about how accurate electronic line calling really is. Bring back human eyes—with three challenges per set. Let the game breathe a little. Most people don't realize that to become a great chair umpire, you first need to be a great line judge—that's how you gain the experience. So, how are the next generation of chair umpires supposed to get their training if line judges don't come back? And if we are going to keep the electronic line calling, here's an idea: let tournaments use the voices of past players for the Electronic Line Calling system. Then, run social media contests where fans can guess whose voices were used in a particular match. The winner could receive an instant prize, and during the next changeover, announce the winner's first name along with the name of the former player whose voice was featured. It would add an extra layer of fun and entertainment for everyone.

Coaching? Embrace It

Done well—and broadcasted—on-court coaching adds strategy and depth for fans. Let's stop pretending tennis is a one-person show. It's a team effort now: coaches, trainers, physios, parents, agents etc. Let's acknowledge it and move forward.

Bottom line: Tennis doesn't need a revolution. But it does need to evolve. A few smart tweaks could make it more compelling, fairer, and healthier—for everyone involved.

Grand Slam Tournament Innovations

I love the US Open's mixed-doubles format and the Australian Open's $1 million one-point tournament – both give great exposure to the majors and are entertaining for fans. I would tweak the mixed-doubles team-selection criteria: automatically qualify the winners of the three Grand Slams that precede the US Open (Australian Open, Roland Garros/French Open, and Wimbledon), then fill any remaining spots by moving down to the finalists, semifinalists, etc., when a winning pair has already qualified by taking multiple majors. That approach rewards consistent Grand Slam success and keeps the event competitive and meaningful.

Share More Pet Peeves? I'd Be Happy To!

- **Let's give women more visibility**
  On sports apps and tournament sites, me's scores and draws are almost always listed first. Why not alternate or display both equally? A little visibility goes a long way. FYI: Wimbledon did it in 2025. So proud of them!

- **Tennis coverage is unbalanced**
  News coverage—whether in print, online or on social media—still leans heavily toward men's tennis. I'd estimate 70% men, 30% women, if that. It's time to even the score.

- **Equal prize money? Not quite!**
  While the four majors offer equal prize money, most tournaments on tour do not. Here, the income gap between men and women in tennis remains significant. Tournaments outside of the four majors allocate more money to the men especially at the 250 and 500 levels. A bright spot: Mr. Ben Navarro offered equal prize money at his WTA 500 event in Charleston in 2026, matching the ATP 500 level. Thank you, Sir!

- **Battle of the Sexes**
  Let's call this what it was: a disappointing spectacle. The Nick Kyrgios – Aryna Sabalenka exhibition in December 2025 lacked quality tennis and atmosphere and it did nothing to advance the sport. It's unrealistic to treat men's and women's competition as directly comparable — physiological differences in strength and speed mean outcomes won't be the same. You wouldn't put the women's 100m world record holder against the men's and expect parity; by the same logic, many male Division I college players could likely beat top women pros. In that match Kyrgios seemed to be toying with Sabalenka rather than competing at full intensity, which made the event feel meaningless and, worse, diminished the historical significance of Billie Jean King's "Battle of the Sexes." King's 6–4, 6–3, 6–3 victory over Bobby Riggs mattered far beyond the scoreline; let's not allow exhibitions like this to cheapen that legacy.

- **The left-handed advantage is real—and rarely talked about**
  As you well know from reading this book, I think it's time we address this built-in edge that's long gone unexamined.

- **Too many top-ranked players in the commentary booth**
  While I respect the legends, we also need more diversity in voice and background. I can tell you from experience that lower-ranked former players often have relatable stories and insights that connect better with everyday fans. Let's hear from a broader range of voices.

- **Tennis and Pickleball don't need to fight**
  They can—and should—coexist and grow together. There's room in the racquet world for both.

- **We need more female coaches**
  On both the ATP and WTA Tours—and across the industry—we need a better balance of coaching voices. A mix of male and female guidance offers players a fuller, more nuanced perspective.

- **A serious issue: sexual abuse in tennis**
  It exists, and it must be acknowledged, addressed, and prevented. The conversation should be ongoing—in clubs, schools, federations—and include education for parents and young players. Safety is non-negotiable.

- **Let former players stay involved**
  They have wisdom to share. Former pros

should be hired more often to mentor younger generations and stay active in shaping the future of the sport.

- **Still undecided on best-of-five**
I've spoken earlier about possible changes, and I'm still on the fence. With younger audiences used to faster entertainment, will 4+ hour matches keep their attention? Obviously, if it were anywhere near as entertaining as the 2025 Roland Garros men's final—a 5-hour, 29-minute epic between Jannik Sinner and Carlos Alcaraz—my new format would be working. And for that matter, I would have loved to have seen the women's final go best-of-five that year too. The match between Aryna Sabalenka and Coco Gauff was so competitive and exciting, it deserved the same stage. It's time to seriously consider some modern alternatives. I would add that regardless of the score in the first two sets both women's and men's semifinals will be played three-out-of-five sets. Mostly for the fans paying exorbitant amount of money for these matches.

- **The men's serve is overpowering the game**
Maybe it's time to raise the net a few inches or allow only one serve per point. Pick your moment for a blast; otherwise, rely on placement and variety.

- **Doubles etiquette matters**
When there's no referee, let your partner call balls on their own sideline. Too often, I see players at the net calling balls out from a diagonal angle—

they're just not in the best position to judge. If you're not looking straight down the line, let your partner make the call.

- **Let players show a little more emotion**
  We love fist pumps and celebrations—but we can also relate to frustration. My friends and fellow commentators Kevin Skinner and Karine Quentrec (former world No. 50) believe players should be allowed to express themselves a bit more without being penalized—as long as no one gets hurt. For example, maybe players should be allowed to launch one ball into the stands per match. Why not? The game has become a little too sanitized. Fans love emotion. Again as long as no one gets hurt.

- **Pre-match interviews? Not so useful**
  Kevin's take? They're pointless. Players are locked in, focused, and often give little more than generic responses. Maybe it's time to skip them.

- **Post-match interviews—let the fans ask the questions**
  Kevin and Karine had a brilliant idea: allow vetted fan questions from around the stadium to be read on the big screen by the on-court host. It would create a fun, personal moment and bring fans closer to the players.

- **Keep the backboards!**
  Every club should have one. And if yours doesn't? Build it. Trust me—they will come. 😊

Martina Navratilova with Sophie Amiach

Sophie's Picks

Best Shots by Individual Players Through Multiple Eras

1st Serve:

Elena Rybakina, Aryna Sabalenka, Serena Williams, Taylor Fritz, Jannik Sinner, Ben Shelton, Giovanni Mpetshi Perricard, John Isner, Pete Sampras

2nd Serve (Kick):

Aryna Sabalenka, Elina Rybakina, Alicia Molik, Sam Stosur, Taylor Fritz, Dominic Thiem

Best Serve-and-Volleyers:

Billie Jean King, Evonne Goolagong, Martina Navratilova, Zina Garrison, Ash Barty, Rod Laver, Boris Becker, Pete Sampras, Stefan Edberg, John McEnroe, Pat Cash, Pat Rafter, Roger Federer

Forehand:

Aryna Sabalenka, Madison Keys, Naomi Osaka, Serena Williams, Juan Martin Del Potro, Roger Federer, Joao Fonseca, Jannik Sinner, Francisco Cerundolo

Forehand Inside-In & Inside-Out:

Aryna Sabalenka, Steffi Graf, Bianca Andreescu, Carlos Alcaraz, Jimmy Arias, Andre Agassi, Roger Federer

Forehand Dropshot:

Bianca Andreescu, Katerina Siniakova, Alizé Cornet, Aryna Sabalenka, Ons Jabeur, Billie Jean King, Carlos Alcaraz, Corentin Moutet, Hugo Gaston, Benoit Paire, Fabrice Santoro, Carlos Alcaraz, Roger Federer

Backhand Dropshot:

Aryna Sabalenka, Ons Jabeur, Alizé Cornet, Kristina Mladenovic, Ash Barty, Anastasija Sevastova, Roberta Vinci, Francesca Schiavone, Billie Jean King, Martina Navratilova, Corentin Moutet, Hugo Gaston, Benoit Paire, Fabrice Santoro, Roger Federer

One-Handed Backhand:

Diane Parry, Francesca Schiavone, Carla Suárez Navarro, Amélie Mauresmo, Justine Henin, Richard Gasquet, Stan Wawrinka, Roger Federer

Two-Handed Backhand:

Victoria Azarenka, Coco Gauff, Veronika Kudermetova, Aryna Sabalenka, Madison Keys, Jessica Pegula, Amanda Annisimova, Victoria Mboko, Chris Evert, Novak Djokovic, Jannik Sinner, Carlos Alcaraz, Andy Murray, Andre Agassi

Slice/Underspin Backhand:

Ons Jabeur, Bianca Andreescu, Monica Niculescu (and forehand & most unconventinal) Anastasija Sevastova, Ash Barty, Roberta Vinci, Francesca Schiavone, Steffi Graf, Martina Navratilova, Pam Shriver (and forehand), Billie Jean King, Novak Djokovic, Rafael Nadal, Roger Federer

Forehand Volleys:

Ash Barty, Billie Jean King, Martina Navratilova, Roger Federer, Stefan Edberg, Pat Cash, Pat Rafter

Backhand Volleys:

Ash Barty, Billie Jean King, Martina Navratilova, Roger Federer, Feliciano Lopez, Stefan Edberg, Pat Cash

Swing Forehand Volleys:

Zina Garrison, Monica Seles, Iga Świątek, Aryna Sabalenka, Jelena Ostapenko

Swing Two Handed Backhand Volleys:

Maria Sharapova, Monica Seles, Aryna Sabalenka, Jelena Ostapenko

Swing One-Handed Backhand Volley:

Roger Federer, Grigor Dimitrov, Stefanos Tsitsipas

Dropshot Volley:

Bianca Andreescu, Kristina Mladenovic, Ash Barty, Billie Jean King, Martina Navratilova, Roger Federer, Fabrice Santoro, Benoit Paire

Serve, Right-handed:

Pete Sampras, Andy Roddick, Juan Martin Del Potro, Marin Cilic, Sam Querrey, Nick Kyrgios (including under arm serve), Roger Federer, Novak Djokovic, Jannick Sinner, Carlos Alcaraz, Serena Williams, Sabine Lisicki, Ashley Barty, Elena Rybakina, Aryna Sabalenka, Zheng Quinwen, Clara Tauson, Linda Noskova (*)

(*) Not including players 6'8 and above

Serve, Left-handed:

Rod Laver, Roscoe Tanner, John McEnroe, Goran Ivanisevic, Rafael Nadal, Denis Shapovalov, Ben Shelton, Jack Draper, Martina Navratilova, Monica Seles, Angelique Kerber, Petra Kvitova

Return of Serve:

Novak Djokovic, Jannik Sinner, Alex De Minaur, Andre Agassi, Jessica Pegula, Aryna Sabalenka, Iga Świątek, Victoria Azarenka, Serena Williams

Best Court Coverage:

Coco Gauff, Iga Świątek, Jasmine Paolini, Lois Boisson, Alizé Cornet, Caroline Wozniacki, Agnieszka Radwańska, Novak Djokovic, Rafael Nadal, Carlos Alcara, Jannik Sinner, Gaël Monfils, Andy Murray, Alex de Minaur

Mental Toughness:

Björn Borg, Novak Djokovic, Rafael Nadal, Roger Federer, Chris Evert, Coco Gauff, Victoria Mboko

Most Athletic:

Serena Williams, Coco Gauff, Lois Boisson, Gaël Monfils, Carlos Alcaraz, Jannik Sinner

Vertical Leap:

Gail Monfils, Roger Federer, Pete Sampras, Yannick Noah, Coco Gauff

Trick shots:

Roger Federer (tweener), Yannick Noah (tweener), Mansour Barhami (the tennis form of the Harlem Globetrotters) Hsieh Su-Wei and Fabrice Santoro, the two tennis magicians